Only By His
GRACE

volume one

JAMES L. BOLDEN JR

Copyright © 2016 by James L. Bolden Jr

Only By His Grace
volume one
by James L. Bolden Jr

Printed in the United States of America.

All pictures featured in the book are the sole property of James L. Bolden Jr.

All graphics, including the cover art were designed by LaShawn Davis."

ISBN 9781498474054

All rights reserved solely by the author. The author guarantees all contents are original and do not infringe upon the legal rights of any other person or work. No part of this book may be reproduced in any form without the permission of the author. The views expressed in this book are not necessarily those of the publisher.

Unless otherwise indicated, Scripture quotations taken from Scripture quotations taken from the King James Version (KJV)–*public domain.*

Scripture quotations taken from the Holy Bible, New International Version (NIV). Copyright © 1995-2010 Bible Gateway Zondervan Corporation Used by permission. All rights reserved.

www.xulonpress.com

ACKNOWLEDGMENTS

I would like to give a special dedication to the people who were very influential in my relationship growth with Father God and in my personal life change:
    Evelyn Briggs "Mom Patty "
    Elder Walter Washington Wise
    Pastor Edna Thompson Murray

To My Family –
    My wife, Erica
    My daughters, Ashley Holland and Toquana Jones
    My son, Karon Demby

To my Mother Carolyn Jones, and my Brother Donnie Bolden

To My Inner Circle –
    Jeff and Ann Butler
Terry and Felicia Travers
    Lamont and Crystal Lofland
    Kyle and Erica Hawkins
    Papa (Jesse) and LaShawn Davis
    Reginald Robinson

To Pastor Larry and Retha Tucker, my mentors and so much more.

To all of my partners and friends of the ministry along the way; thank you for your support and experiences.

*Special Acknowledgement to LaShawn Davis, my "more than an editor", who received a box of scrap papers, sticky notes, and spiral notebooks, and over the course of two years fashioned those into the book you have before you today.

ABOUT THE BOOK

This project is carefully and cleverly crafted by God the Father. Its purpose far exceeds simply being a "good read". The revelation and experiences have been recorded over a 15 year period of time and reads more like a book of Proverbs and Psalms, than a typical chapter book. In fact, we don't have chapters, we have "endeavors". While deciding what the divisions of the book would be called (chapters, was not an option), God spoke to my wife Erica, the word endeavors. After getting a formal definition, we agreed that it fit perfectly what the book represented. Vocabulary.com defines it as: a purposeful or industrious undertaking; especially one that requires effort or boldness. We believe that chapters end, but endeavors move easily from one to the next.

Through this book we invite you to take a journey; a journey of self-evaluation that will challenge you and provoke change.

After the entries, we have provided a "Journey Journal" for you to take notes. The purpose of the journal is so that you will have a written record of the insights that Father God will reveal to you as you read.

Please note that we are aware of any and all grammatical errors. We felt that in order to maintain the integrity of God's word, to and through the author that some things were best left unedited. Also, note that wherever the pronouns are capitalized (Me, My, His, Him etc.) it's a reference to God, and not the author.

Understand that through this book, it's not our job to tell you anything, but rather to lead you to the One who can show you All things.

Let your journey begin...

WHAT'S INSIDE

Acknowledgements v
About The Book. vii
Scripture Reference. xi
The Inspiration xii
Prayer xiii

Endeavor One – Grace 15
Endeavor Two – Matters and Motives of the Heart 41
Endeavor Three – Just Be. 81

2 Timothy 2:1-10 NKJV

BE STRONG IN GRACE

Y ou therefore, my son, be strong in the grace that is in Christ Jesus. [2] And the things that you have heard from me among many witnesses, commit these to faithful men who will be able to teach others also. [3] You therefore must endure hardship as a good soldier of Jesus Christ. [4] No one engaged in warfare entangles himself with the affairs of *this* life, that he may please him who enlisted him as a soldier. [5] And also if anyone competes in athletics, he is not crowned unless he competes according to the rules. [6] The hardworking farmer must be first to partake of the crops. [7] Consider what I say, and Lord give you understanding in all things.

[8] Remember that Jesus Christ, of the seed of David, was raised from the dead according to my gospel, [9] for which I suffer trouble as an evildoer, *even* to the point of chains; but the word of God is not chained. [10] Therefore I endure all things for the sake of the elect, that they also may obtain the salvation which is in Christ Jesus with eternal glory.

THE INSPIRATION

Yearning To Love

I have to/Yet I must learn to grow more and more in love with Him—this is my place, this is my access to life and that more abundantly, even eternal. I have to make Him—Let Him—Yield to Him, in/at all times with not just His place, but His love, to be my center—The middle—The interior. God the center—me as His tabernacle of love. Then and only then is He my true defense!! I can let my guard down and His fortifying Spirit surrounds me, from the inside out and outside in. His love is my protection. I need Him; I need His love more and more. I need Him to show, manifest, His love towards me, His effectual fervor concerning me, that I in return can show, manifest His love, His effectual fervor towards Him and others.

PRAYER

Father, give to me this day, Your love, the increase of Your love. That I be wrapped up and consumed; increasingly swelling, ever seeing my everlasting love!! Your loving approval; that's all I want. To gain much, love much and to receive much-love.

Can we put everything down for a minute or more and let love be the center?? Real love!! In Him, For Him, From Him. {Receive to give}

Breaking through hindrances... Trust TRUST

December 23, 2003

God is so good, so awesome, that He stands obedient to His own will. His own self: His will is so perfect that it/He causes you to be and follow His will/His self. John 17. Jesus sanctified Himself.

He sent (gave) His Son in the form of Himself and to be obedient to Himself, His will. (Perfected Holiness)

Man can't rule His own spirit without God, for it too, is God's.

June 2, 2004

For one of the first times I look at what God wants from me and out of me. I'm kinda like scared by it, because I cannot do it. I have to let Him do it and I don't even know how to do that. I fear Him, and yet, the one thing I do know is I "have to" trust and have faith in Father. Even in where we're going and what He is going to do for us. Where He wants to take us.

Journey Journal

October 25, 2004 12:00 am praying

It is alright to walk in the boldness of the Lord and in confidence, without sinning.
There is a certain fear that people have that keeps them from this place; a spirit of failure/fear.

Yes, the world and other Christian saints will question this. It's My chastisement that keeps you and will keep you even in the matters of boldness and confidence.

Your confidence and trust is in Me, My Son and My Spirit, My grace and mercy. Learn to grow in it, to gain in it, to oversee many wonders I'll give unto you. Stand!! Having done all that you can do to Stand. Stand therefore.

Ephesians 6:13-14 KJV

[13] Wherefore take unto you the whole armour of God, that ye may be able to withstand in the evil day, and having done all, to stand.
[14] Stand therefore, having your loins girt about with truth, and having on the breastplate of righteousness;

Only By His Grace

⚜ *Journey Journal* ⚜

July 17, 2006

His Grace is Sufficient

Just when you think you've got it, His grace shows you a higher way of thinking and redirects your focus on a higher manner/standard (kingdom way and kingdom standard). Man's advancement then comes through God.

April 22, 2008

Bumble bee
Come to pollinate not sting

I got startled and feared when I saw the bee, not identifying what type of bee it was and that it didn't come to do any harm.
To pollinate is to bring new life and new season.
That's what this ministry is and is to do through God and His grace.

Journey Journal

January 21, 2006

Inducting Grace to be Fulfilled

The standard is bible and word based. God has a way of inducting the instructions of His word into our homes and our lives. He inducts Himself and His word into our homes and lives in many different ways, at different times. The times are different from one to another.
(He gives, He takes away)

Man has to be very sensitive to God's movements during these times and seasons. We have to be sensitive to God, and to ourselves concerning what role He is to play. We also must be sensitive (complementary) to others; knowing God's movements and being sensitive to what He's inducting in our homes and in our relationships with others. We must communicate with God to gain understanding and relationship that will bring revelation, grace and mercy to our homes and lives. Now our responsibility to grow in relationship with God and others has gotten greater. Allowing freedom, not fear or strife, but grace, to be filled in our lives.

Journey Journal

Only By His Grace

February 17, 2008

The closer we get to God's grace, the more effortless it becomes to complete what God has purposed and ordained in our lives. The closer we get to God's presence, the intimacy of God, the less of a carnal effort is exerted and more of a faith effort.

Have faith in more of Him and less of us, our carnality and fleshly doubtful thinking. Obedience in faith to His instructions that gives us the ability to complete a task and to fulfill prophesy and scripture.
He spoke a personal word. Obedience equals faith matching God's spoken word(s).

"Yet Everything is for our Learning!!"

When the glory of God shows up or is evident in us and shines through us, the less human effort it takes for us to project and produce –Fruit of God/ results/manifestations. Yet God also assists us in our human effort. God's perfect will or being out of His will: Which one do you want?? God's grace will be evident in the lives of those who *will* carry and who *are* the carriers of the glory of God. (Take notice of the testimonies of these people)

They will not be accepted or sometimes even noticed *because* of their lack of effort according to the standards of men. (Men's structures, schools and theology or interpretation of how grace, mercy, etc. are supposed to come or be, and what we are supposed do to obtain them) Once *ob*tained, they are not to be *con*tained, but to be let free.

2 Corinthians 3:17 KJV Now the Lord is that Spirit: and where the Spirit of the Lord is, there is liberty.

This is where we will see the True manifestation of God's glory; when we let Him be free in us; through us. Allowing and noticing those He sends. The Carriers.

Heaven comes to release, He sends His carriers for a release!!

Call; Ask God; Make the call for those who are sent to bring forth and release the glory of God!!

These are a particular people; specific people. Yet full of integrity, faithful, trusting in God and Him only shall they serve. They will not be without character, they are groomed by God's Spirit.

Release God, Release the Carriers!!

Only By His Grace

Journey Journal

Only By His Grace

November 16, 2012 11:00am

The area, characteristic and/or thing that you hold on to the Most, is the area that Father wants to have; that's the area you must surrender. We've been conditioned to automatically look at what we're going to lose when we're presented with a thing or with what we have to "give" up. But even a good business man looks at the profit or gain in a thing in both cases.

Romans 12:12 NIV Be joyful in hope, patient in affliction, faithful in prayer.

Because we only see in part and haven't been re-conditioned, we become scared. Fear kicks in the door of our progress through selfish manifestations and the union between faith and grace doesn't emerge. We stop and justify with what we call rational justification, not knowing that *now faith* can't be built it must be manifested. And it can't be built upon, except through God's grace.
(God gives us each a measure of faith)
All of our good, best, great ideas
were manifested by faith!!

Can we give up to gain? Can we continue to go through the process of renewal/reconditioning to higher heights and deeper depths? That the union of what is truth in us and in our lives manifest-now and through faith!! Not manipulated by the hands of man, but pure in heart, pure in thought, pure in deed. Truth=Success.

Matthew 5:8 KJV-Blessed are the pure in heart: for they shall see God.

Only By His Grace

⁌ *Journey Journal* ⁌

June 10, 2004

God's legal way of helping people is still through people, by giving birth to His Spirit *in* a person. He's still reproducing Himself. The development and growth of the attributes of Jesus in us depends on us allowing God's Spirit and will, to grow in and out of us.
Even by our choices in Him and obedience through faith.

From the beginning to eternity God is still reproducing "sons".

Thank you Father, Thank You Jesus, Thank you Holy Spirit, Thank You Holy Angels

September 14, 2014

God's grace is sufficient in things and through of all His names. His grace covers all languages and definitions of His truth, as long as your heart is stayed on Him.

Journey Journal

August 6, 2006

My question:
What must I do to submit myself to You (Father God) this day, surrender, that Your will, Your perfect will be done?

Father's answer:
Give mercy, where mercy, grace and forgiveness, are due; that you may gain mercy, grace, and forgiveness. That brings the heart of compassion of God!!

Give, that you may gain the more to give. Give, that you may be filled with My glory!! Bring life!! Bring love!!

Usher in the very heart of love and life. Given to receive and received to be given. Exchange!!

Journey Journal

February 3, 2006

With growth comes change!! You can't say, "I've grown" and not changed.
- Matured change
- Responsible change
- Healthy and upright

Can you live life looking forward (ahead), and not looking behind to find anything good or bad? But embracing all of what God has placed in front of you. All of the newness that keeps you walking toward and looking to Him; and challenging you to grow and obtain that which God has ordained in your life?!?!?!

Even that which will walk you into His Glory!!

Forward Motion! Not to capture or contain a situation or event that God has done or fixed in your life; but to be lived. No turning back, No regrets, No disappointments in yourself, other people or in God. A *right now* faith life!! A life full of joy, peace, love, and a sound mind; to be experienced.

Only By His Grace

✑ *Journey Journal* ✑

May 30, 2010

Don't look for a new work, but hold fast to what I've given.
Let what I've given line up with and enhance
what I've said!! Where the Spirit of the Lord is,
there is liberty.

God leads, He doesn't drive!!

April 15, 2007

When I come to the truth, I have an understanding.
Whatever part that is being revealed to me, that's where
my true understanding is. It's not getting an understanding
then truth, but rather getting truth to have understanding.
So I wait,
ponder, wrestle, question, commune with the Lord to
get truth that brings real understanding of
kingdom's way; kingdom's standard.
Once understanding, I see clearly and I know my way.
I'm fully persuaded in truth.

Journey Journal

November 14, 2010

It is the *Need* that causes pursuit!! The Need is in Him, you are the value; you are valuable to God!!

**Falling in Your Arms Father, What does that look like?

Being completely vulnerable and submitted to My will. Completely. Having no control; surrendered to the situations and circumstances that you can't do anything about. (Jesus said I do nothing of My own) But give it to the Father and fall in His arms. Even in what He has ordained and told you to do. Not seeing until that exact time, as Isaac did, being sacrificed.

Reflections= Abraham + Isaac; Father + Jesus

Journey Journal

Only By His Grace

April 13, 2005 8:00 am

I want you to be so totally dependent on Me, so that you are continually in a vulnerable place in Spirit and Truth.

Not leaning on your own resources, but God and in all of His treasure in Heaven! To live out of the treasure of Heaven, being dependent on and vulnerable to the Father!!

In this you'll know and learn; in all of the experiences I give you.
I will not have you ignorant, but enlightened in joy, in Spirit and Truth!!

July 28, 2009

The key now is to continually seek and find God inside of us and allow what we find (Him) to be as Big as He wants to be. Once we learn to love and reverence what's (who's) on the inside of us, we don't have to keep coming up with different things to do (performance) or ways to find Him!! (Keep seeing Him on the inside) Seeking.

Journey Journal

Endeavor Two
Matters and Motives
of the Heart

May 20, 2008

We want God to give us His heart, but we haven't given Him our hearts. We haven't cleaned or allowed His cleansing of our hearts, because a veil is still over our hearts. Not knowing and understanding as much as we want Him and His heart towards us – He wants our hearts and yet He still gives first.
(God already has – we haven't or we're still trying to)
You can't fall when you're kneeling to the Father.

"Exchange"

By the measure of love we walk and live in, in our lives with God the Father; That's the measure of power that is made manifest in us.

When it's raining you can't work, yet things still grow. (In the field) Are we going to see as God see's or continue to see as we see?

Only By His Grace

❦ *Journey Journal* ❦

Only By His Grace

December 3, 2007

In the movie the Passion, Jesus says, "Father, my heart is prepared". There is a place that the heart has to be prepared to endure the walk to the cross and to handle the glory of God. Only God knows the heart of a man, so there's a place where no man can teach you, it can only be done by His Spirit, His preparation, His teaching.
It goes deeper in His word, deeper than His word.
God's life, God's desire, God appointed, God's reality, taking on in your life.
No man can teach or prepare you for that!!!

Heart to heart with God—Chest to Chest with God
Breath to Breath with God
Life taking on Life

Having great compassion for
A dying people; A dying race; A dying nation

Deep calling on deep
Being apart of Him, Being apart of His Son
Becoming a Son, True Son's/Sonship

Father Your Perspective takes me beyond all understanding.
Thank you Father; Thank you Jesus; Thank you Holy Spirit

Journey Journal

January 29, 2008

Follow through to the land where love prevails.
It's in our hearts where we connect with the heart and will of God. Deep calls out to deep. The love that God has stored in the depth of our hearts, is where we must go down into and allow the compassion to rise. To go with, to follow through with God into ourselves, our heart of hearts, to see where we really stand.
To see what true love is.

Can we take a look? Are we ready to look inside of us? Are we ready to handle the beauty of God on the inside of us, our hearts coming forth??

It's like the men with the talents. Are we ready for the full expression of God's love to manifest, through our attitudes, character, and emotions?? It's time! But aren't we somewhat scared? It keeps us vulnerable to God and to people.
It will also expose your heart, character, attitude and emotions. We get to the truth of the matter, those hidden things. They come up and come alive in some cases, but must be freed, dealt with, and in some cases, put to death. (Crucifying the flesh and all fleshly attributes)

All with You Father, Your Spirit, Your help. That we may properly
and pleasingly serve You and You only.
That we may properly and pleasingly present ourselves; our hearts to you.

Psalm 51 KJV

1 Have mercy upon me, O God, according to thy lovingkindness: according unto the multitude of thy tender mercies blot out my transgressions.

2 Wash me thoroughly from mine iniquity, and cleanse me from my sin.

3 For I acknowledge my transgressions: and my sin is ever before me.

4 Against thee, thee only, have I sinned, and done this evil in thy sight: that thou mightest be justified when thou speakest, and be clear when thou judgest.

5 Behold, I was shapen in iniquity; and in sin did my mother conceive me.

6 Behold, thou desirest truth in the inward parts: and in the hidden part thou shalt make me to know wisdom.

7 Purge me with hyssop, and I shall be clean: wash me, and I shall be whiter than snow.

8 Make me to hear joy and gladness; that the bones which thou hast broken may rejoice.

9 Hide thy face from my sins, and blot out all mine iniquities.

10 Create in me a clean heart, O God; and renew a right spirit within me.

11 Cast me not away from thy presence; and take not thy holy spirit from me.

12 Restore unto me the joy of thy salvation; and uphold me with thy free spirit.

13 Then will I teach transgressors thy ways; and sinners shall be converted unto thee.

¹⁴ Deliver me from blood guiltiness, O God, thou God of my salvation: and my tongue shall sing aloud of thy righteousness.

¹⁵ O Lord, open thou my lips; and my mouth shall shew forth thy praise.

¹⁶ For thou desirest not sacrifice; else would I give it: thou delightest not in burnt offering.

¹⁷ The sacrifices of God are a broken spirit: a broken and a contrite heart, O God, thou wilt not despise.

¹⁸ Do good in thy good pleasure unto Zion: build thou the walls of Jerusalem.

¹⁹ Then shalt thou be pleased with the sacrifices of righteousness, with burnt offering and whole burnt offering: then shall they offer bullocks upon thine altar.

What can we do or what are we doing, if our hearts aren't right? If we have not allowed God to continually explore our hearts motives and intents
toward Him and His people??
When exploration stops——- Trouble!!

Journey Journal

January 21, 2008

Holiness is keeping the truth sacred in your life!!
Identifying that which has been defiled by the enemy modified/updated and institutionalized by man; and getting back to the heart of God and Godliness.
Truth- Holiness-Righteousness

February 14, 2007

All of Heaven lives in full confidence of the Creator, not even taking into consideration the loss of anything given to them. (Not even life itself)
Do you want Heaven on Earth?
Jesus told Pilate no man takes my life but I give it.

John 10:17-18 KJV [17] Therefore doth my Father love me, because I lay down my life, that I might take it again. [18] No man taketh it from me, but I lay it down of myself. I have power to lay it down, and I have power to take it again. This commandment have I received of my Father.

Jesus said this in John 6:39 NIV

[39] And this is the will of him who sent me, that I shall lose none of all those he has given me, but raise them up at the last day.

"No one" can snatch anything out of His hands.

John 10:25-30 KJV [25] Jesus answered them, I told you, and ye believed not: the works that I do in my Father's name, they bear witness of me.

[26] But ye believe not, because ye are not of my sheep, as I said unto you.

[27] My sheep hear my voice, and I know them, and they follow me:

Only By His Grace

²⁸ And I give unto them eternal life; and they shall never perish, neither shall any man pluck them out of my hand.

²⁹ My Father, which gave them me, is greater than all; and no man is able to pluck them out of my Father's hand.

³⁰ I and my Father are one

Matthew 16:25-NIV ²⁵ For whoever wants to save their life will lose it, but whoever loses their life for me will find it.

Matthew 10:39-NIV ³⁹ Whoever finds their life will lose it, and whoever loses their life for my sake will find it.

Matthew 6:25-33 KJV-²⁵ Therefore I say unto you, Take no thought for your life, what ye shall eat, or what ye shall drink; nor yet for your body, what ye shall put on. Is not the life more than meat, and the body than raiment?

²⁶ Behold the fowls of the air: for they sow not, neither do they reap, nor gather into barns; yet your heavenly Father feedeth them. Are ye not much better than they?

²⁷ Which of you by taking thought can add one cubit unto his stature?

²⁸ And why take ye thought for raiment? Consider the lilies of the field, how they grow; they toil not, neither do they spin:

²⁹ And yet I say unto you, That even Solomon in all his glory was not arrayed like one of these.

³⁰ Wherefore, if God so clothe the grass of the field, which today is, and tomorrow is cast into the oven, shall he not much more clothe you, O ye of little faith?

³¹ Therefore take no thought, saying, What shall we eat? or, What shall we drink? or, Wherewithal shall we be clothed?

³² (For after all these things do the Gentiles seek:) for your heavenly Father knoweth that ye have need of all these things.

[33] But seek ye first the kingdom of God, and his righteousness; and all these things shall be added unto you.

To Be Transformed By Such a Love, that it so greatly radiates from you, that those around can't help but notice and yet not even want to do you harm.

And even the enemy of such a love,
recognizes it and has to respond to it.
It will drive him away or he will want to do harm to you.
(that kind of love has discernment with it)

Journey Journal

March 16, 2005

No matter what the difference is, can you support the vision of another under the counsel of God, so that one day they will support even your vision? "The Cross is not a comfortable place!!"

February 20, 2004

The "Pure" at "Heart"

It doesn't look for ulterior motives. It doesn't look for doubt, failure, disbelief, cunningness, craftiness, or disappointments.

It doesn't set itself up. It looks for honesty. Its motive is honest; Its intent is honest!!

It doesn't look for opposition, even though it's there. The honesty, love, focus of power and spirit of it, goes through opposition. The attributes of it flows around and through anything and everything.

It knows itself, looks for itself, goes after what it's sent for and accomplishes its intent.

Journey Journal

May 18, 2008

You'll know when change is pure; You'll know
when the heart is pure. The guidance and instruction, the
leading is by Me, by My Spirit!!

Know what is pure and holy, it comes by My Instruction,
My guidance. For the pure at heart shall see Me!!
Learn the ways of purity!!

Not an emotional stirring, but a Spiritual stirring.
Uncontainable, Uncontrollable, Unconditional

June 4, 2003

We become grown (grown-up) when we not only take
responsible for our own lives and those around us, but
when we take on the responsibilities for our own lives,
and those God has placed around us.

Take care, with care, giving care,
sharing care.

A way to tell what's in a person's heart is for
God NOT to tell them anything and see what they stand for.
What choice will they make? (to be with us or without us)

Journey Journal

March 3, 2004

As long as we keep our focus on (heading towards) our salvation, our relationships will always be intact. We'll always keep God first.
—Maintaining the standard in us.

Respect and love
Respect is to cherish. Cherish is to keep. To love, respect, and/or cherish our relationships, means that we choose to do what it takes lawfully, spiritually, mindfully to keep them.
We cling to them because they become special to us and we don't want to lose them. Keeping our hearts pleasing to God through faith keeps us away from reproach.

Faith concerns itself with things that are honest and true. It's meaning, It's living; It's a living Spirit.
We try too much to prove our faith to people!!
Be quiet sometimes! Let God prove Himself.

Journey Journal

May 10, 2010

In a relationship, even with God, we're looking for
Something God has not given yet, or promised.
What is our expectation?
What do we want in return for our goodness;
our good deed??

Is it health from God or our own self-righteousness?
Who do we want to give us the reward?
So what or who are we looking
at as our rewarder??

We can look for salvation in many different
ways (places, people and even things).
But if we and our homes aren't right,
we'll never find true contentment. Often we find
ourselves content in (settling for) things that God
never intended. True contentment can
only be found in Him.

Likewise, we'll never find that real truth of salvation
we are or we have been looking for!!!

᪥ *Journey Journal* ᪥

May 14, 2010

Instead of trying to get Heaven to respond to us, we need to wait to see what heaven is doing and then respond to what Heaven wants and is doing.

We're looking at our own patience and tolerance instead of looking at God's/Heaven's patience, and tolerance for us.

Waiting for Heaven to recognize and approve of us even in what God has said. Instead of acting out, promoting something, and/or doing something outside of the character of Heaven.

Finding peace (inner) and cooperating with the true nature of Heaven. Having patience and tolerance of all things, knowing we have something in common, that we don't lose
our dominion, yet and still, not taking another's.

Harmony would be what I see Lord!! Along with true freedom in its smallest form to its largest!!
Dominion- to rule, to reign, to have power, strength, to make-"without doubt"

Journey Journal

August 11, 2010

I've been doing too much thinking, rationalizing about what God is and has shown me, instead of praying concerning what He has to say and what His heart is towards the matter. Seeking His solution about the situation, not my knowledge, know how, or even my biblical "spiritual" stand point.

October 13, 2004 7:00

In the midst of everything, find Me. I'm teaching you to seek and find Me in every situation and circumstance, without fear or trembling of the situations and circumstances.

Journey Journal

February 22, 2007

We have to be mindful that in your times of being hospitable, that we don't put yourself in the stead of God!!

We must check our heart's motive and intent towards the people we're entertaining. That intent must always be for them to meet and/or get closer to the Father.

They're not coming to see us, but to meet and see the Father. Not man, but God. Even though He uses men!! Where's your heart in this?!?!

—Learning to love: A heart of love and worship—

Only By His Grace

◈ *Journey Journal* ◈

October 16, 2004 9:36am

Our sacrifice is not what we put on the altar, but what we let go!! It's not a sacrifice putting something on the altar, it's a sacrifice to let go of what we put there.

When Jesus was on the cross, Heaven closed up. God had to let it go, to see it through.

Getting there is one thing, letting go to see it through is the nature of man's problem. I'm also adjusting the nature of man in My ways, from corruptible to incorruptible. Corruptible nature fights and strives against God's plans and purpose because it can't see the use, the hope, or the way of God, Man can't see in faith.

The incorruptible nature presses for the will of God. Keeping us in tune with the plans and purposes of God, to the leading and working of our faith. Exercising the very heart and nature of God's Spirit to completion.

Seeing it through to keep pressing for the mark of the high calling which is in Christ Jesus.

Journey Journal

October 24, 2004 8:40am

Life's challenges and victories are NOT our testimony, it's Jesus' testimony.

It's not how we made it through, but how Jesus got us through.

We keep our eyes on the fact that it's not our testimony, but Jesus making the testimony of our lives unto Himself.

We will begin to see our controls are taken off. He's the navigator of our lives. All that comes is of God's creativity and of the testimony of and in His chosen and given life in us.

What or who the Father has given, no one can take away. None is lost. No one can pluck out of His hands.

He's the author and finisher of our faith. He is the creativity of our lives. Seeing reality, seeing Jesus, gives greater courage and confidence in our walk, in our calling, in our overcoming, in our endurance of situations and circumstances of life.

We're not the focus, but the will of God, the creativity of Jesus, and the Spirit of truth that leads in this greater testimony.

Only By His Grace

⸎ *Journey Journal* ⸎

November 27, 2004 4:04 am

I want my Father- I want my Father to bless me, make provision for me, manifest these things for me because of my situation and circumstances.

So my focus and heart's motive is not on Him, but what He has.

My focus and hearts motive have got to be that "my Father" will and has already provided, because of His Word! Not because of circumstances and situations.

So my belief and faith is in the wrong place of focus. Stand on "His Word" and "His promise". Fast for focus of faith, strength in faith, belief in faith, manifest power of faith.
Revelation and wisdom in and of faith.

Journey Journal

March 18, 2004

We look and search after God for our individual being and purpose. But do we then think on or search after God's purpose for us as a body, as a whole in our homes, church, and jobs? Even in our extra-curricular activities?

Broadening and or opening our eye's to more. Changing our outlook on our life, family, job, activities.

Finding God's purpose or what He wants from our particular church, family, job. We'll find a new sense of prospective and purpose.

Ask ourselves the question: God, what is Your agenda for my family-church job activities? What do You call my family, church, job, activities?

Journey Journal

February 20, 2005 5:00 am

A river overflowing, a stream in the midst of the gardens. How can he preach unless he be sent. I will cause favor to come upon you!! This you will know.

See and experience without trying to understand. See and experience=let revelation come in; embrace and receive-understanding is given.

Clearer-no striving-all trusting, brings deeper, clearer meaning. Keeping a pure heart.

May 19, 2005

"Heart of Compassion"

Let your heart affect what you see, not what you see affect your heart!!

October 12, 2008

Father, we thank You, and we welcome You with open arms. We come in celebration that today we are the sons and daughters of God.

That in this celebration the expression of Your love and joy and Your heart be made manifest. And the fulfillment of Your heart and will be done.

In the name of Yeshua the Christ we pray, Amen

Journey Journal

April 8, 2016 8:30am

Once the Ministers of Satan have caused someone to take on certain characteristics and attitudes, their assignment is up.
The attachment is there.

That's why we must allow Father and His counsel to prevail in and around us.
We must allow His Word to be exercised in us.

Our follow through is a continual practice to bring not only *victory* and *subjection*, but also the beauty of Righteous Relationship.

The Growth continues: Defeat to Destroy!!
We break generational curses, we destroy old habits, corruption, unrighteousness and unhealthiness.

We let go the old man to destroy and bury its works. By Fathers Spirit, this is the accomplishment He gives us.

Do we and/or can we Trust and have Faith?

Only By His Grace

༄ *Journey Journal* ༄

Endeavor Three
Just Be

January 21, 2003

(Believing in yourself)

If nothing else, believe God for His ability in you.
Then you can get on with believing
in your ability in God.

October 28, 2004 7:15 am

I find that there are different focuses and
desires that try to trip up a man
or woman.
But it's not about what comes
to try you; it's about how you allow
God to adjust your spirit,
mind, and heart to overcome, even
the more greater,
that which was trying you.

Journey Journal

March 2, 2004

"Growth"
Go beyond just living God's word. Let God's word become you. Become your natural being, your natural ability, attitude and way of thinking. Without doubt and questioning who you are and what you're doing. (You'll know when you're outside of yourself or God's spirit) We walk it, talk it and sometimes live certain things.
Is that really who we are?

Do we Let God and God's anointing, grace, and mercy, loving kindness, fruit of His Spirit, consume us and even over take us in our walk it, talk it, live it experiences; our living? Just being who God created you to be and knowing that, and as much as God have given you at this time?!

Acceptance- of the kingdom of God and all therein

Acceptance -of your place in the kingdom of God

Acceptance -of who you are in the kingdom of God

Acceptance -of what you are to do in/
for the kingdom of God

Thank you Father, Thank you Jesus, Thank you Holy Spirit, Thank you Holy Angels

Journey Journal

March 2, 2004 4:10pm

Let God make, mold and shape your ambition, and ideas. Your drive and your willingness to do whatever He has first purposed you and given you to do and or be in this life!!

In prayer- 5:30 pm
Let what God has spoken in your life—become your life!! Scripture: Psalm 138:8 The Lord will perfect that which concerneth me;

October 8, 2001

It's not that God doesn't give us what you ask for, some things we ask for, that are according to His will, we have to be prepared for. That's where waiting comes in. God is not going to give us something that's going to corrupt us. So He will prepare us for it.
WAIT on God's preparation;
The more we do, the more we begin to look for and see God!!

Journey Journal

October 29, 2003

You have got to see that God is real in your own way, for yourself,
no one can do that. (In your experiences, in your life, in your relationship with Him)
How do you relate God with your life and/or your reality?

-Righteousness or Unrighteous
-Holy or Unholy
-Peaceful or lacking peace
-Joyful or lacking joy

Romans 14—Staying out of judgment

Do you see Him (God) for who He really is or do you see God for what your interpretation of Him is and/or what you think? Do you esteem God to be *more* than your interpretation/ *more* than your thoughts? If you don't pursue to see Him, (who He really is and what He really stands for) then you will develop and have a false sense of who God is and that falsehood will be easy to believe!!

Psalm 119:104 KJV Through thy precepts I get understanding: therefore I hate every false way.

Only By His Grace

Journey Journal

Prayer

Lord, keep me away from the devils false interpretations, false manifestations, false duplication of Your work, Your will, Your word, Your glory. In Jesus name

When you know that you know, hold on to that which is real, that which is truth. My Father's response:
I will forever be your God;
your King, your Father, your provider.
Not as man has, or in man's ways.
But according as I have purposed in My heart,
in My word, in My commands

When you sense the presence of the enemy;
look for the table of God

**Let me ask you a question that religiosity can't answer: Have you ever really identified or recognized one of God's chosen?? Would you know him or her if they didn't come exposing their identity?? If they weren't saying they're teachers or identifying themselves by titles or positions??

Every day is ushers day. We're all created to usher in the Spirit of the Lord!!

Only By His Grace

Journey Journal

April 5, 2005 12:18 pm
(A glimpse into my personal struggle)

Well Father, I'm tired of trying to justify, defend, give an answer or rational excuse for what You have told me to do or for how my life is.

People are always trying to fix me. They have more formulas and analogies to fix a person than You do, so it seems.

Trying to keep up with giving an answer of understanding to them- I'm tired-
All of what I can give, is it really worth it??
They still see what they want, they're locked in.

I'm tired of the fight, of even being offended, it does me no good with You Father.

I find that my attitudes of defending myself, and my faith, are not so good, but bitter.

Justifying what You say and have said to me, having to give or prove understanding, like I know and have it all together, is beginning to be not worth the trouble. And pushes me into overthinking.

I understand and know
it pushes me towards falsehood and over analyzing what You have said.

It's like they think I'm too young or too dumb or don't have enough understanding; or that You don't give understanding with a word.

It's alright not to know and/or even see something at times,
until you reveal, open, pour out or give.

Like You or me are too dumb to do Your work and
I'm too dumb to receive Your word with understanding,
and know what You would have me to do at that time.

And even in what I don't know and or don't get exactly
right, that it's alright because You're there and Your word
will prevail. (That's what freedom looks like)

All things will work together for the good of
them that love the Lord, I love you Father
because You first love me.

It's sometimes like we can't believe, trust, or have faith in
You and that be that-without being questioned or doubted,
even mostly by believers.
Not encouraged!!

I have to believe in You Father for the great
and little things in my life, natural and spiritual.
According to the measure You have given and told
me; to stand, I can't turn back.

I've seen and know, I have believed and trusted. I've tasted.
If I am a fool or foolish, I will be that for You Father and
You'll have me to be and/or raise me above all.

I have faith and trusted, believed with all
my heart, spirit and mind, my Father, my Lord,
my God, my Jesus. The revealer of truth even
through foolishness.

Only By His Grace

So Father continue revealing Your truth to us as a people as a whole and individuals, I thank You!!

Even to build the maturity to know how to handle and deal with these matters as You will! Spirit and word; personal and corporate.

The battle is not ours!! It's Yours Father!!
Thank You Father,
In Jesus Name, Amen

Journey Journal

October 28, 2003

Our problem is that we don't believe that God has been, has done and is already. He doesn't repeat. All you are, is already done. Our job then is to be obedient and believe and have faith in what God has said and is saying; to act or do what is His perfect will and pleasant in His sight.
(Believe in the Already, I Am)

We keep falling back, because we don't believe we're ahead.

January 25, 2005 Morning Worship

Embrace My love, My wisdom, and My fruit by the Spirit, not to capture with the mind. The expressions of My will and My heart in what I've created you to do, and who you are in Me, will freely flow.

Embrace Me by the Spirit, capture Me in Heart, freely receive, freely give, in Me, to Me = in you, to you. In others, to others.

Freely flowing in My Spirit, My love, My word.
Be at one with My Spirit;
Be at one in heart.

Journey Journal

December 19, 2009 Thoughts

The more God shows me or teaches me, in one another, I find that there are other area's that I can't see. And every now and then He gives me a collective view of what He has shown and taught me.

Yet I can't hold it all, view it all, or teach it all without Him!! There's always something that we don't know, understand or see!!

I have to be mindful of this. I learn it through my wife and daughters. My expectation is greater with them and sometimes that's not a good thing.

I have to "Just Be" with God, my Daddy, to sit at His feet. Not get caught up, even in my own theology and view.

How often do we do this?

~ *Journey Journal* ~

*Thoughts

I'd rather run to see what God has or to see whether God's lying, than to stop and see that He is true. So in other words, I'm not ever going to stop running.

Romans 3:4 KJV Let God be true and every man be a liar.
Numbers 23:19 KJV God is not a man that He should lie.

April 24, 2005

Spirit/Angel of the Lord said- God didn't give you all that He has given for you to
back up and quit!!

November 18, 2004

Sometimes you don't need to Do anything but
Be there.
"You be and I Will"

Journey Journal

September 9, 2010

Today I heard the Lord say," It's not about what you can do, but about waiting on Me!! Stand still and see the salvation of the Lord" My Pop Pop used to say:
Psalm 27:14 KJV—Wait on the LORD: be of good courage, and he shall strengthen thine heart: wait, I say, on the LORD. Even though I have spoken, there is a period of time you still must wait for Me!! I find that when men don't know what God is doing, their desires (Ideas) of working or doing takes precedence.

The anxiety to do something for God, for ministry, causes us to think of something, or our desires and ideas begin to even answer for us. Especially our religious ideas and our own theology and righteousness. I find that's where we must be careful and Just Be!!

Letting things (blessings, wisdom, the fruit of God's Spirit) find us. Letting the blessings come overwhelm and over take us. Can we wait for what He has sent??!!?!

Only By His Grace

❧ *Journey Journal* ❧

October 21, 2010

It's not all that easy is it?? There's a responsibility you must approach and keep!! Go back to the foundation of the matter.

Matthew 5:8 KJV—Blessed are the pure in heart; for they shall see God

2 Corinthians 3:13-18 KJV—[13] And not as Moses, which put a veil over his face, that the children of Israel could not steadfastly look to the end of that which is abolished:

[14] But their minds were blinded: for until this day remaineth the same veil untaken away in the reading of the old testament; which veil is done away in Christ.

[15] But even unto this day, when Moses is read, the veil is upon their heart.

[16] Nevertheless when it shall turn to the Lord, the veil shall be taken away.

[17] Now the Lord is that Spirit: and where the Spirit of the Lord is, there is liberty.

[18] But we all, with open face beholding as in a glass the glory of the Lord, are changed into the same image from glory to glory, even as by the Spirit of the Lord.

January 15, 2005

I have heard your prayers and your cries and I have blessed them, go and fear and doubt no more!! For I AM the Lord thy God.

Journey Journal

October 23, 2010

When we go higher in altitude the oxygen (air) gets lighter, and our thinking gets distorted. We must recognize this and get in the Spirit!! So that we stand strong, still thinking rightfully, righteously.

Our flesh has no discernment. No ability to make rightful decisions.

January, 31, 2006

The key to obtaining the no disappointing anointing is having total trust and faith in the Father, in His word, and in His promise over us. (The battle is not ours, it's the Lord's)
Isaiah 61:6,7

*Father, we thank You for helping us overcome the negativity and giving no place or opening for the enemy!!

January 19, 2005

Father I want to live and see the vision of my life, to be experienced (revealed), and shared with You. In Jesus Name. Amen

Journey Journal

November 5, 2004

(Wisdom- The things of God- Fruit of the Spirit)

Knowing is one thing, coming into the maturity of what you know through the experience of living, is another. This maturity brings greater belief, trust and faith in what God has shown or given you; mostly wisdom and/or revelation of Him.

Knowing how to use what you have makes you more effective (vision, dreams); letting them become you and who you are.

March 9, 2004

Do you not think that when you enter in (worship, praise, presence), that I don't know what your condition is? Am I not big enough to overcome, even that, with My love, to teach you??
"Wine Press"

Journey Journal

January 26, 2005 Morning Worship

Father You set the tone of freedom. Father You govern Your praise and worship. Father You set the order of Your praise; Your worship; Your service.

Where is Your freedom? What is Your freedom?
Unhindered

Do we understand? Really and fully?

There's release when we're free.

What are Your expectations this day of me?
May I see?

Order Your freedom – Govern Your freedom.

Stand to let freedom reign in Your people. Stand to let freedom reign in the body of Christ.

To see the realness of Your liberty; To see the truth of Your true worshippers.

Where freedom is!! What freedom is!!

Let freedom reign Father, Let freedom reign!!

How do You see it Father?
What is freedom?- Unhindered love, un-orchestrated expressions of our heart and love; and God's heart love.
We must endure!!

A true worshipper is not moved by a person's response. We are moved by His response!! Do not look for it, just be.

No one dictates that.

I look towards you Father in all things and I give you thanks.

Thank you Father for understanding, for wisdom, for revelation in getting me us through every hindering factor; to be free and freely give Your liberty.
Let it reign in us Father. Thank You, Amen

It is work to be free and stay free. (Galatians 5:1-18-25, 13)

Only By His Grace

⁂ *Journey Journal* ⁂

April 12, 2005

Doing and being what's pleasing to the Father will always keep you in tune. From the very beginning of seeking God, I always prayed; "Lord I want to know the truth not by man but by you!! To know the truth and speak the
truth and live in truth." Knowing that there may be something we're missing in God. How we perceive Him and His ways and statues.

There's a way we think, plan, etc., that causes us to miss God and obtain the things of God. To see them living and working in our lives and in others' lives.

Proverbs 3:5-7 KJV
⁵ Trust in the LORD with all thine heart; and lean not unto thine own understanding.

⁶ In all thy ways acknowledge him, and he shall direct thy paths.

⁷ Be not wise in thine own eyes: fear the LORD, and depart from evil.

Do we really believe God?
Our formulas, methods, and books on "how to", are getting us wrecked, because we don't give room for the change that God wants to bring. God doesn't need our help!!

He's not stupid!! He knows all. He's beyond figuring out, but we try, even to fix people and to obtain to contain. Just when we think we have, God does something to "BOOM", blow our minds!!

Maybe He does that on purpose!! Let God be; In all His ways, in our lives!! Believing and trusting in the truth with "all", fully having faith in the Father and His truth.

Only By His Grace

∼ *Journey Journal* ∼

November 17, 2005

The Father puts us in certain places and under certain conditions, not only to teach us, but also to bring things out of us (good and bad). Be mindful not to get judgmental and complain about your surroundings not knowing that God put you there!

December 18, 2003 1:30pm

The work of establishment of God, is not in buildings or places, but in us.

Psalm 90:16-17 Let thy work appear unto thy servants, and thy glory unto their children.

[17] And let the beauty of the LORD our God be upon us: and establish thou the work of our hands upon us; yea, the work of our hands establish thou it.

Journey Journal

December 30, 2003

Come to the knowledge of and belief that you don't have to *become* super natural-you are supernatural. I abide in you and you abide in Me. That which is in Me IS supernatural.

Don't let the devil try to tell you to go or strive to obtain more than what you already have. (or what God has given you, ordained, equipped you with)

—When you're in the will of God, you're living out the Lamb's book of life. You're living out of what has been written and living out what's to be written. You're living new testaments. You're not just reading Bible, your living bible.

What you do for God, and how you live for God is being written in the Lamb's book of life. Being recorded in Heaven!!

—BE sure about yourself and your ways!! Live in My Peace. Disobedience and uncertainty, the irritation is for you to Identify being outside of My peace and My will!! Get back in My peace, live in My will, My perfect will, that you remove uncertainty and doubt.

—Return to your first (true) love

The true essence of this is: God is trying to get you back to the state in which Man was originally created. That's how God first created Adam. Your first state is to be like Jesus.

⧞ *Journey Journal* ⧞

December 30, 2003

Jesus said that He came to give us life, and *that* more abundantly. I just found myself with a life joyful smile. I thought, "I'm finding life". The more I find myself content with God and in God, the more I find His peace and love.

He sits over me, I realize I'm findng life. I find I'm loving life with all that comes. But I'm no longer afraid, because my confidence is in my Jesus, in my Father, in my God.

It's joyful seeing in Him, through Him, to know I don't have to be afraid of anything that may come. And knowing that my Father will be with me, in me, around me, protecting me every step of the way.
Guiding me, instructing me, chastening me, in His Spirit; with His Spirit. Glory Hallelujah

Journey Journal

July 3, 2003 1:20pm

The more you believe in God, have faith in God, trust in God, the greater your deliverance!!

**Having Joy... that we can praise You and worship You, do Your will, not in fear of what the enemy can do and has done, but in joy of what Heaven can bring!!

October 12, 2004

Once you receive in your heart, you no longer have to study to make yourself to be, you live to be.
You live it, it becomes you!!
The Law and His word!!
In Spirit and in Truth, Just Be!!

Journey Journal

July 30, 2010

Wake up with Joy and keep joy and hold onto joy.
Don't let circumstances, situations, people, places, or things
give you joy. Quit looking for something to give you or make your joy. That's a false joy, not God given. His joy is given within, from the beginning. Look forward to and for your joy!!
Let your joy guide (build) you!!

In God, with God, in your day, every day, keep your eyes on it!!
Change! In joy, with joy.

**At the end of everyday God has commanded even the sky to come at peace. So will we!! There should be a time every
day that you take and come to peace with God, yourself, everyone,
and everything in your life! Bring everything under subjection to Peace.

Journey Journal

April 25, 2016 2:00am

Discipline is the major difference between most religions. Some have a natural discipline in their religious practices.

So the question that I see is: Can we discipline not only our natural lives but also our spiritual attributes, ways, character, and attitudes?

We have to have discipline and dedication to the right focus (righteous focus), pay attention in relationship and communion with Father and His Kingdom.

The continuation that leads us to Heavenly places is having "Righteous Desire". It's that growth that takes us from faith to faith, glory to glory and brings us into the Truth of Father. Righteous desire ensures a right (Righteous) relationship with Father, Son, and Holy Spirit and the Host of His Kingdom.

Are we meant to evolve or Just Be? Restoration should be a part of our focus, not evolving.
But being restored into the Being that the Will of the Son and the consent of the Father created of Himself and gave to be shared.

Because He so-loved man, He wanted *all* of His creation to love what He did; All His Kingdom to *adore*!!
That's the place and the being that I want to return to/ be restored to.

That's life worth living, that's worth finding out, seeking for, and even *dying* for.
Being what He created to Love.

Only By His Grace

Allowing The Father to be well pleased with what He
Created in the likeness and
image of Himself.
(So I smile just writing this)
The Father is allowing me to see and
feel just a little of His Heart in
this matter. Yet knowing He's not
going to allow us to get home just
any kind of way.

It's His way or no way and in *that*-
is His Grace.

What do we want?
What are we looking at
or for, when we consider who we are,
and who we want to be?

Are we looking at the way the world and
all its influences view and tell us?

Are we really seeking to find Fathers Heart,
Will, and Way for this life?

What He wants for our reality for real?

Now Patience and Faith must be renewed and restored in
us. Growth given through Grace
that the Father pleases Himself through us.
Then let Him share as He pleases.
(Just another smile)

Joy!! I feel the Joy in my Spirit that flows in my natural.
We've got to get this and allow Father to build that we live
even eternal. Amen. Thank You, Father: That we have the

access that You have given us into your Grace. The pleasure of Your Creation, Your Love, Your Worship. In the name above all names; Your Son, Your Holy Spirit. I (we) give Thanks, All Thanks. (allowing Father to get our attention and we keep paying attention. That's our Cost).
Attention Span Growth!!

Journey Journal

Only By His Grace

Journey Journal

Journey Journal

Journey Journal

Journey Journal

Journey Journal

Journey Journal

Only By His Grace

Journey Journal

Journey Journal

CPSIA information can be obtained
at www.ICGtesting.com
Printed in the USA
BVOW11s0549250616
453411BV00002B/3/P

9 781498 474054